No. 25

Geraldine Clarkson

Shearsman Books

First published in the United Kingdom in 2018 by
Shearsman Books
50 Westons Hill Drive
Emersons Green
BRISTOL
BS16 7DF

Shearsman Books Ltd Registered Office
30–31 St. James Place, Mangotsfield, Bristol BS16 9JB
(this address not for correspondence)

www.shearsman.com

ISBN 978-1-84861-615-8

Acknowledgements
Grateful thanks to the editors of *Shearsman, Tears in the Fence, Iota,
Magma, Live Canon Competition Anthology 2017, Smiths Knoll, Under
the Radar, Envoi, Primers Volume 1 (Poetry School / Nine Arches Press)*,
and *nthposition* in which some of these poems have
previously appeared.

Special thanks to Arts Council England for their generous support in
enabling me to prepare this chapbook, also to all who have commented
on these poems, and particularly to David Caddy and Ahren Warner
for their thoughtful editorial advice.

Supported using public funding by
**ARTS COUNCIL
ENGLAND**

Contents

Lovely the Leam and her sisters
milling through Midlands
watermeadows. Broadbacked
and elegant, halving the Spa town.

There was a story in childhood
of three daughters of one family,
adrift in a boat, lost. Leam lowered
her gaze and mourned. Hypocrite river.

RIVARIATIONS

I *The Ouse Is My (Unexpected) Home*

I slip into the day as into swish silk.
Up before anyone, digging out morning's
moist newness like truffles. Green prickling
my nose, sharp as thorn. I head down the slope.
Hop. Down by the apple trees, down by
the apple trees. Skip.

The water is plated, a table set for tea.
One little white teacup for you, my dear.
A trembling, almost transparent, slice
of angel cake.

Icy green slink—*oh why did you*—
fugitive flurry, rattlesnake breath.
How roomy here, in this black heart.

II *Louis Limpopo Laments*

like an oiled clarinet, a bouncy bassoon,
with caulked cork on his back. A sulky slider
of green treacle, slow, with a sloe-gin kick,
all from one lung. Through desert and forest,
he's hippopotamussy. Has one ancient urgent
push to carry me home. Fever trees
make a low chariot. *Ain't going to
study war no mo'.*

III *Shelagh Shannon Shoulders the Cross*

She batters rocks like crockery, brims.
From overhead (the familiar home-tug
gets you from all angles), you see she trails a mane
of porter-black, with its froth, and gullies of
ginger, jellied air. What did they all
want, my sorrows drowned. It's goodbye,
Muirsheen Durkin. *Going to lay down my*
burden, down by, down by. Pulling up
through bog and moor, potato land. Gliding by
strange new settlements, shiny acre gardens. Old
hurt. Work away now, work away. These rocks
seep secrets. Rough words into the night.
Someone who oughtn't to be there. Lies.
Something wrapped in a cloth entrusted
to the emerald stream.

IV *Mr Derwent*

How d'you do, my rushing gent, tawny-capped,
whiskers bristling, up at Howden, busy about
a northern agenda, along steep corridors,
ten thousand items to see to, circling the scree
and sparing a word to court the lady scar. Debrief
at Hathersage, healing rush down through
Matlock. Thick oak valleys. You try to hold it back
but you break out with such a brown surge.
Whip, slap. Mutate, flower into cotton and silk.
I follow in my head, on, on through rock
and lime and moor, always forward
with canny grit; brief circuits, blunt as a tongue.
The wind confounds you at Ambergate.
I spent two years trailing you
then wonder where you went.

V *Gave de Pau, Lourdes*

One leap down from the snows, and she pauses the tune
to pass the shrine—rheumy, watery place. Milk-green
with the sun on it, rising, full of lace.
October firebombing the trees.

So cold. The shock of contact—mother's blue
obliterates thought. Baby's legs working, treading air
in a jig of anticipation, little life held close, nut-heart
refixing itself to the tree, held hard, one flow.
Now nothing new will ever be the same again.

The House Dreams

began when the house was sold. I returned nightly without fail. Once, there were new owners and we spoke different languages. I stopped at the front garden. Another time I sneaked in, and had to be abject when the lady owner came back and seemed affronted. One weekend I went and slept in my old bed, luxuriant, fearful of Monday. The worst, I was trapped in the bathroom, her voice rising the stairs, getting nearer, her hand on the ivory plastic knob, and I woke to protect myself. There was a life-size crib in the back garden, containing my father. Scenarios unrolled with my mother and people I'd just met, in the kitchen, and a partitioned quarter of the living room. I met someone injured in the street and told the ambulance driver to take them back to the old house (the new lady not impressed). Real life, I was told that everything went wrong for them, gas, water, garden, electrics. The most haunting, I am searching under the floorboards, there is damp black earth, and treasures, blue-and-white fragments, I am excited, knowing these will be valuable, too, to my sister. She refuses to look.

Sons and Fraughters

Duty fully placed plates on the table.
Dutifully placed plates as she was able.
Dutifully spoke after spoken to.
Dutifully hung around, burning.
The Jury came down against.
Jewry was implicated.
An imp was created.
Duties conflated, a goblin lived in the roof.
Little women stitched hems.
Moo-cows plumped around the field, in clover.
A whole decade was spent training the house not to bend.
A man fell asleep after work, singed his socks.
Things were moist or dry and had to be combined.
Wishing was a shirking vice.
Boys came in from football late, were given sandwiches.
Dusk had furry fingers.
A man sang all day, tunes lifting, making the rafters hop.
Schleech. Schleech. Went the baby.
A clockwork dog defecated near a white picket fence.
The moon yodelled the women.
A man grew up to be a woman.
A woman faltered.
The moon cooed.
Fridays, friends came, but only of the men, for milk pudding
and fish.
Saints were a part of it. Standing saints said *this*; sitting saints, *that.*
There was a lifting in the leaves each springtime.
Food was plentiful, joints torn apart by the men, blood dripping.
Summer stank but had a beautiful archway under which they
played late.
They carried stones to make a wall, brought sand from the beach,
foundations were unsettled.

Let us straighten the house.
Autumn ravished the women with smoulder and mould.
Winter, hail. A railing from above. Some of the women bailed out.
Walls began to dissolve and the house ate everyone
except for a baby which had been placed under the floorboards,
                                            for that night only.
The house left the floorboards alone.
The baby was brought up by dog-goblins and learnt to spell and
                      dedicated herself to straightening the house.
When she was 7, she gave herself the name Duty.

A Thursday

Attendant circumstances: the sun and the moon, in that order. Running home, no reason to think the house would not be as we'd left it. Mother wiping workaday hands on her stretchy pink overall. Father gulping down tea, talking to whoever was there, his soft-steel presence filling the house, so that we breathed in, moved carefully into corners. And my brother: thinning, staring, wandering off for longer and longer, forgetting to say where, just flushed cheeks and eyes shining like polythene. But the noise coiled through the windows and walls before we arrived—a wind of tangled voices sighing and soughing. The back door open. Mother not in the kitchen. Father, loitering. The next room quickly dark with cousins, uncles, Irish people, all *here* not there. On top of each other, two heads to each person. All the heads crying. And Mother by the fire, flanked by four aunts. Someone took us to a back room, away from the sobbing-wind sound, offered us sweets, as many as we liked, while day turned to night, in that order.

Lament, My Natural Home

How curious the hedges, cut back and boxed,
trimmed and moulded like poodles; alpines
regulating their borders.

The roar of Cashmore is stilled to a hiccup,
a whimper. No baby's cry, or whiplash
mother's complaint, no ruckus

of brothers teasing, or father singing
'King of the Road', low, melodious,
as he works. No car bits outside the back door,

no jack or wheel, or spare back seat. No old
carpets growing mildew in the shed.
The garden ends, which never ended before,

with patio and pretty beds. The hall is shorn
of overcoats. The walls glossed, coffee tables
glassed. No-one is dying in the front room,

of a hacking cough, while *Home and Away*
plays out its credits. No-one in sight. These were
never rooms for solitude. I wore you

like a cloak, patterned with geraniums,
and spider plants, lily-of-the-valley. I looked up
at the stairs, mountains winking in moonlight,

hinting at futures. When everyone had died,
when everyone had gone—I waited that long—
I wore you like a cloak, a snow-mantle to hide me.

I wore you like armour for fighting grief;
for self-oblation. Finally I offered you up
as involuntary sacrifice. These strangers

have stolen our space. They rent living
quarters while we have whole hearts rent.
They lack our native knowledge; lack kin.

Spinster Soup

Thin *consommé,* in a *drip,*
drip, pippety-pip,
apple-pip,
soft, poached ovaries
& retrenched cherry-stone
nipples. Dried meat, jerky
with desire, simulates breasts,
shoulders, haunches, salted,
lightly spiced. Salsified
tongue, thickened
with mealy lentil-based
language, conditionals
like *I would have, I could have.*
Stale ciabatta legs.
The whole laced with brandy
and angostura bitters.

On the Street

Here you are, a feast
of breast, offered the
lady with ginger hair.
All autumn, burning
auburn lit the street
and painted her
into every awkward
corner. Ornamental. Hips
on the hedgerows
triggered 3-D pictures
and dragging longing.
I did what I could to
resemble a Japanese
maple, matronly and
dragon-tongued and pert
as heaven. Ready to seize.
Caesar, she called me.
I made eye-contact.
Chrysanthemums'
scuttled petals
like gold fivers perching
in both gutters.
There, there, she said.
Gives, gives.

Filth

(after ten days)

Mult mult mult mult. Orange light
invades the street. Prayer is hung
in quartos. Idle eyes calculate the damage
of ten nights since his long blue-suited limbs
unfolded from the carapace sepia interior
of a 1950s sedan, his pointy face
anxious and private. A pall of tragedy
about his ears. How he approached
the front door where mild suburban weeds started up—
doubled wires dipped in violet. 'Bella Langley?' he probed.
'Some news of your son.' Mult. The pipit face broke
into ricochet smiles and frowns. Mult? 'Come in.'
The soft pandered atmosphere made way
as the deranged house urged him in. Doors
double-locked. Curtains folding him into promises
and blood oaths. Silence burrowed through the neighbours'
walls. No-one emerged. Nothing until the sirens, the lights.
A blue suit stained. A caged bird. Microbial activity.
Sympathy cards. Mult mult mult. Mass-produced
prayer. Sepia photographs under rank multiplying
headlines. *Belladonna*. Appallment. Violet light masters
every unshaded window in the street. Mult.

Hopeless on Hope Street

Hope lopes along like a bandit.
Mrs Molesworth looks sceptical.
Wants the streets cleaned up. What a pass
when every low-looking male
can stuff municipal waste bins with white stuff
to believe in. Outside the barber's, Hope
combs a moustache and finishes with a gloss
of wax, taking care to equalise left and right.
Mrs Milkwater expostulates that low-looking
girls can air their toilette in public as if
at a show. She gathers up Hope's implements
and secretes them in her handbag like hotel
courtesies. Mannequins stand in protest
outside the town hall, 17 abreast, reaching
as far as Bell Street. Their gaze favours
the right side where shop windows
are spritzily lit and sparsely furnished.
The man watering the Council flower baskets is dazzled,
transported to the Russian ballet, light on his feet
as he leaps past, illegally snagging aubretia
from solicitors' window boxes. Hope stifles
a cough, lifts a muffler. Mrs Merryweather
desteams her glasses and considers the ways
in which peace will come, by water
and by blood. False sunlight falls hard.
Hope struts on high heels. The street
is busier now. Flesh in flux. The evening
is a belter. Lights stuck on red. People singing
hymns at the zebra. Some men are cursing
their lives while women wonder about
crossing. Some set off together; sometimes
they drift back, swaying.

Eyes in a Whirl

On the nth of suck-tuber, an ounce and a pinch of thyme,
two mothers in the same gown of blue burlap,
were passing the new pig-five block near the park
on the bus. Eyed each other: *Get off and lark it!*

They gathered musk and bourses, eggy,
and peeped themselves on two flues. Text-fawning,
they hit the egg-sack. Summer was not sealing the gorse
but an old shrew, with cool enough plinth to smuggle

to Ipswich, laughed off neonatal silk. A stud
cajoled them with a mouthful, and Winnie,
the second mother, free-ranging the cursed time,

rolled over in lavender, staggered up smelling of roses.
You wronged my ex, claimed Dr Mitry, her co-player,
sore lover. *So pin it, and draw it, and scram!*

Mother's Meals

Fag ash sprinkles the spuds as she peels, intent. On the stove behind, a half-dozen pan-lids ring and hop, cymbals in her queendom of cabbage, halibut, and steam. Podgy roasts of pork, beef, and lamb bloom under her gaze like orchids, nudging hunks of parsnip, carrot, marrow; onion ¼s. Our education through her cooking: nursery-rhyme lists of ingredients recite themselves, blend to make cows jump over the moon. Child-picked mint and wild horseradish stand by for spoon-standing sauces. Huge-dumplinged stews and casseroles twine smells to lasso every room at late afternoon, before being heaped implausibly high, on double bunk beds of mash, on plates colour-&-size-coded for men/boys, women/girls. And then a ½-alphabet of crimped pies, crumbles, and tarts—we learn to spell by eating them—apple, apricot, blackberry, blackcurrant, cherry, damson, elderberry, fig, gooseberry, greengage, mulberry, pear, quince, rhubarb, strawberry, Victoria plum—yellow pastry tumbling into sudden steam, and making the rafters sing 40-verse ballads with fiddle accompaniment. On the sideboard, optional courses—modules in pleasing and being pleased—melon crescents, meringues, flans with jellied mandarin and glacé cherries; extra-curricular custards, junkets, flummeries, blancmanges, Instant Whip; Carnation milk; eloquent trifles, well-spoken sponges; Irish soda bread, French toast. We aspire to graduate to the serious sweets—yds of milky macaroni, tapioca, semolina, sago and rice puddings, with thick nutmeg-brown strokable skins; final exams, suet puddings steeped and steaming in crock basins—with lemon, ginger, candied peel—poetic and adrift in philosophical syrup, treacle, molasses; mathematical conundrums of acute-triangled bread-&-butter puddings, geometrical Chelsea-bun spirals, roly-polies, and upside-down creations; evolutionary Eve's, and Queen of, puds; a natural selection of fairy cakes and fancies. A syllabus of syllabubs. All finished with a shake of sugar, cocoa, or mixed spice, and a backhanded wipe round the edges. The ordinary sublime. Knives sharpened on the stone step. Everything bleached after.

Vault

...the lesser light to rule the night (Genesis 1:16)

The periods of the Moon are regular
tight as a bell but tempestuous.

She hurls saucepans, yells, tips cauldrons
of mercury down mountains. Moans.

Won't answer the telephone. She remembers
being called the lesser light and curls her lip.

Her belly keens, her coolness
gone. Calculations flit.

She wakes earlier. Rises in the day
hungry for the Sun. Lets loose her shawl

in rivers of silver all over the sea. Drops pearls
on backs of leaves bared to the sky.

Calls out at 1 a.m. No-one answers. Hints
at self-destruction. Glints brilliant

but trembles, unsafe. Can't speak.
Sees a kid with peachy cheeks out late

playing with her brothers in the street.
Narrows witchy eyes and draws, draws.

The girl's face ruddies as she looks
up: alert, stung.

Whole Salmon

He's a family friend, astounding in emerald and oatmeal, with a clotted brogue and a grizzled pony tail and he's gentled me into a corner, where I pin on a smile which keeps pivoting upside-down and my cheeks have gone scarlet, I've downed too much whiskey mixed with self-censure to recall how to be, and I need a system, yes, for taking one breath then another and even, oh ideal republic, for speaking and walking away, but my neural pathways are dazzlingly blank and unhelpful, and he sneers—*so shy, has the cat run with away it?*—my throat tightening while, all along the length of my gullet, priests and policemen are bracing themselves—*very decorative, but you have no chat... and what d'you imagine the boyfriend's up to now with all the pretty Yankee girls?*—flat country hands paddle the small of my back, my hips, press and withdraw, his nag-tail tangles my crucifix, and nothing ever goes outwards with me, it's all curling back into me like a salmon in spate and you could say that salmon's the problem as he's traditional in bringing a whole one each day to the house, no questions, no charge, and he's a hero for it, an absolute hero, my mother's jubilant, triumphant, not believing her luck and we're all ecstatic, and no-one will ever hear a word against him and *what would you say*, he says, *if anything happened,* and he's being a card, like he is, jack of hearts, a lovable generous rogue, they say.

Unlawful Daughter

This was the dream that held me for years
This was the house that Dad built
This was the shade of lime that we detested
(This, when he died, we tried to preserve exactly)
This was the concrete step lipped in crimson
This was the dead rabbit posed with my nephew
This was the full-frontal tide
This was the start of the story
This was the steely Atlantic that beckoned
This was the bulrush lake
This was the common, fritilla'd with daisies
This was the whore sea which took the Armada
This was the house built by one man, not a builder
This was the other house, not the one we lived in
This was a house of sorrows, green and deep
This was a beacon
This was the poor man's castle's keep
This was not allowed for me to keep
This was snail shell, mirror, container
This was crawlspace from which eviction occurred
This was the swinging blue gate, bolted
This was oilcloth, salt air, mouldy antimacassars
This was misunderstood
This was hard heaven, this was offering
This was cage, soft coffinwood
This was feelings battened under floorboards
This was death-space for Dad, coughed-out-loud
This was fall-space for Mum, alice-like, tumbling
This was my Christmas party dress, resembling curtains
This I haunted after leaving
This I dreamt I sneaked back into at weekends
This I dreamt the owner, hostile and evictory
This many-chambered dream I inhabited like a grave—
in time recording it without comment.

Of Uncreation

The river of poetry—denied a simple mouth,
dammed by ceramic politeness, demeaned into
unmeaning meandering by worthier
workier work—hung back, treading water, while I
wrote letters frozen in courtesy with no guttural
gota, drop (down) to even parenthetical reality,
paper-locked in protocol; deviated into fancy angry emails
darted off to half-known colleagues; oozed into acts of
compassion and compulsion; transuded into acrostic
shopping-lists fluid with vowel music, concrete in shape
(parsnip tapering to a *p),* crammed with similes (plums
as red as cherries) and leaked into nervy songs tricksy with jokes
—turned black, lurched, thundered in my ears, rattled skin till
                                                                it felt
the wrong size, on the wrong body, at the wrong time.

Lorm

Lorm lifts his head
and licks his lower lip
where the woman had laid her hand
and wrist. He tidies himself.

His focus switches, to a forest.
Firelight. Orange faces beam
and sing. Some kind of camp.
And Lorm takes his place, affable.

He has a biting type of humour
sarcastic scissors
that swizzle through
and trim the edges

of the rather wholesome
boy-scout camaraderie.
But it is late at night
and there is beer and wine

and everyone's delighted
at this little danger come
tugging at the leash
the group has twirled about its fist.

By morning, Lorm is sloping home,
that slightly decadent pull
of a full belly stretching
its skin. Whacked. Satisfied.

When my enemy came home with my love,

I was
on the phone. Necking-and-chinning my mobile, I chased them
into the kitchen. My love ended up in the corner. My enemy
between us. Glowing. *Don't give me a bloody hug, then,* I made a
kind of lunge, uncharacteristic. The glow baffled a bit, knocked
to one side, then the other—*puff!...puff!*— the way white flour
in a polythene bag might do if punched. We went back into
the main room and she folded languorous limbs against a long
blue body while she recounted the afternoon they'd had. I heard
about a meal at a deep-bowled place called *Sahn-tah Loo-CHEE-
ah.* A laugh. Delicious giggles like echoes bubbling up from an
Orvieto wine-cellar. In a low voice, some trembling revelations
she'd been party to. Hinted at. Flashes of glow. Here. Everywhere.
A glass shatters. Chaos.

Creeper

That November, my sister kicked
a kitten heel against the stump of ivy
at the old front door, mother gone,
me guarding house. *It's dead, let's*
face it, and you've no business staying.
I ran my hand along the rambling trunk
where red-veined stalks had sprouted
every year since we were children;
now rough and lacking sap. I stroked
its blunted nodes, its absences. It was
a hard winter. The sun stayed low.
I stayed put. In spring,
giant leaves flocked the wall,
thick as felt: you couldn't see
the bricks at all. My sister called
a specialist, who said the tendrils
looked set to rot the mortar. *Look—*
my sister said—*it's taking over,*
bringing the whole house down.

Melody's Meadow

There are flowers out in my head that are still bulbs in the everyday world, tight-lipped. There are always other beds to consider apart from this one in the middle of a meadow, canopied with biblical hawthorn, which we've made our own. Beds within beds, cooled then warmed, decoded. A piano in the hedge, stuffed with old newspapers, which plays when I am asleep though I try to rouse myself to see if it could be a mouse or a melodeon. My parents visiting again, first thing, this time checking why we haven't got curtains, or walls. I try to tell Dad about the piano, he would be tickled, but my pronunciation is way off and he doesn't recognise the words emerging like aubergine. My mother keeps going off by herself, looking for more modern meadows, with self-cleaning daisy carpets and colour badgers. There are at least a dozen other children claiming her care, looking anxious and reedy. My brain is stuffed with laburnum blooms, ravishing but poisonous. We turn to pray and two of my nephews light honey-candles and act as acolytes. One overacts. A sailor on a quest for enough sky to make himself a pair of trousers drops by, but the steel-grey heavens strengthen a tendency to introversion, and no-one entertains him. One of the sisters baptises herself 'Xenophobia'. He asks another sister to marry him and she quizzes him about his clothing allowance. Half-a-dozen brothers scrap for his compass. By this time it's evening and the hour to draw the veil over the bed, twiggy and fragrant. My beloved turns to bestow a kiss but I snatch it from him prematurely, green and unsucculent. I leave it with the sailor, a morsel next to his nightcap. The day has not been as fruitful as others in the meadow but at least there were no marauders, and only a scattering of goats. Two of my brothers shout out, claiming to know where we are.

When tooraloos were taboo,

the old folks crouched in the hedges, soft peat leaking
between their toes, rubber bands curbing their fingers,
in a backspin as they tried to master the new rules.

Their tongues were trained in different shapes
from the ones the government was allowing now,
their throats once oiled with jugs of punch,

knees freighted with pretty wenches, one fine morning
in May... June, or July... by the Mountains of Mourne
or the Cliffs of Dooneen, wishing wishing wishing in vain

to be maids or youths again. Even whistles were
proscribed, and the joyful jig of the accordion
abandoned, which had set knees and heels

reeling and tapping. *She said come in, sir,
and meet my father...* Who knew when a tooraloo
would break loose and what it would do. In the end

you could always escape across the main, as many had before,
too-ra-loo, to *Californ-eye-ay*, and instead of singing praties,
you'd be singing lumps of gold, too-ra-loo-ra-lay.

Unlearning the Cloister

I am baptized by coins with a faint smell of elderflower
—Natalie Lyalin

I am one of the unsaved, lacking coin
and lure of oil; I stagnate,
gaze at one part of my cell then another.

Unholy night shrivels, lies in state:
star clerics concoct black holes in colanders,
stainless steel hearts bend deeply.

I am a novice pepping myself up
with chutney and lavender.
I unpick a pillow, give it a thump

then detach a light bangle
from a lame girl's wrist.
We shuffle together across a province.

Every farmhouse door shuts in farewell,
no bird sounds chirpy.
I stretch my legs and puke darkness,

a lily appears in the back of my head;
yellow shale shifts backwards.
I attend one christening, more than enough.

My body reflects oil, perfectly.
I am full of chill and vim,
like the new ones.

Lustre

I've raggled my tail thinking of her. Gross glister of skin
above drooped stockings. Eyes pissed, her twitching
stick neck. Her caked face all lacework and doughy pasta. I'm
                                     maddened
with why he wants her lumpen lustre when I'm clean and neat
as a tine and faster than he or she and can more than pass muster
in and out in the mornings before they're awake, the master first
and her the last, dreamless till noon, mouldy sister. I've cussed her,
swallow blades when I think how he's kissed her, how he says
                                  like a ninny
he's missed her when she's away, won't know himself for joy
                          when—*basta!*—
he's lost her. By my kind grace.

Nutmeg, America

I arrived in Nutmeg in the fall,
late, as shopkeepers were drawing their blinds.

I arrived in Nutmeg just as shopkeepers
were drawing their blinds, faded blue slats
over dusty sunned windows.

I arrived in Nutmeg. The schoolchildren
were all either dying, or else doing okay,
and being called in from the street
to indigo doorways.

I arrived in Nutmeg to a hollering wind,
the sort that drives the sea into the streets,
and money out of the pocket for supplies
of duct tape, tins of beans.

I arrived in Nutmeg as the Prom Queen '79
was announcing her undying love to
herself in a touching wedding ceremony
on the lower pier. Jellyfish attended.

I arrived in Nutmeg as the sky was turning
Good-Friday black, the sand was puckering up
the beach and flying into my eyes
and armpits like smart sand.

I arrived in Nutmeg as the B&Bs
were boarding up their porches and the *No
Vacancy* signs swung viciously in the wind,
half-unhinged.

I asked for Monica outside a bar, and a frowning
local nodded over to a two-bit, brownstone house
with frowsty doors, and flags in the yard.
Some kind of lily bent back in a bed.

golden opportunity wet streets

give his side a golden opportunity to move
each passing minute seemingly misses one
—if you have
anaconda, or ball python, pine—

opportunity to read what everyone
open in the mouth and good
could see. For one year flowers shone
blooming in Sweden at the end of May.

Assigned to the city of Spokane,
we are over the charred or crumbling
rain-wet street. I stood at the War
(for seconds). Lilies sued for peace

each passing minute seemingly missing one
while lilac snow milled wisdom in city ruins.

oulipo yew engenders TT strop

oily graveside glove shunted. Motto pops.
Cone shape sings, mining tissue
of hay—vie
a dapple, a coin, a thorny *no*.

In pop tryout, a doter overeaten (why?)
a hotdog mound, phone nite,
curdle of slow—nearer—eyes, hoof, nose;
glib moon, dew nines; anatomy hefted.

And, if egoists speak no cot, they
hover, chartered, or—alembic wren-rug—
retrain tweets: the raw iota dots,
forced sons, idle lies. Faeces pour

canapé sighs, gene-slimy, semi-nosing.
Limned owls will leach, ruin Midi sow's icy tit.

Muzzy McIntyre

Muzzy McIntyre brushed her bangs and went pell-mell down the staircase. The banisters pulled her palms back with their waxy residue and the ball at the bottom looked grey-black with grease. This place has gone downhill, she thought, descending. But she went out onto the front step and the mahogany door was flaming—it was that time of day—and the brass lion knocker, brilliant, was shooting out gold spears. All around, the red brick of the houses was deepening. For the sake of these twelve minutes or so, perhaps, one could tolerate the blanched mornings and the puny electric nights; the dust; and critters; the drunken singing of the wind in the passage; the pious crooning of the neighbours. The waiting. Her other self, the slow Muzzy, ambled out to take the air. She looked up and down the street, laid the flat of her hand to her forehead, against the slanting light. Another fine day tomorrow, she drawled, headlocking a memory.